Can't Stop the Feeling, 7 Years & More Hot Singles

Contents

ISBN 978-1-4950-7246-8

HAL•LEONARD®
CORPORATION
7777 W. BLUEMOUND RD. P.O. BOX 13819 MILWAUKEE, WI 53213

Visit Hal Leonard Online at
www.halleonard.com

CAN'T STOP THE FEELING
from TROLLS

Words and Music by JUSTIN TIMBERLAKE,
MAX MARTIN and SHELLBACK

Moderate Funk groove

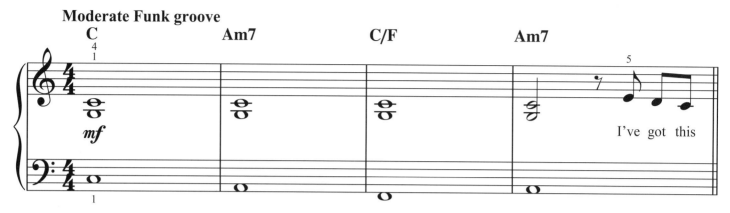

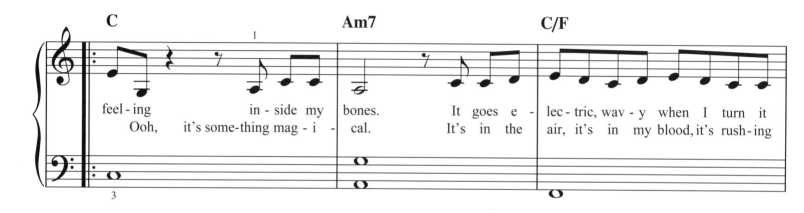

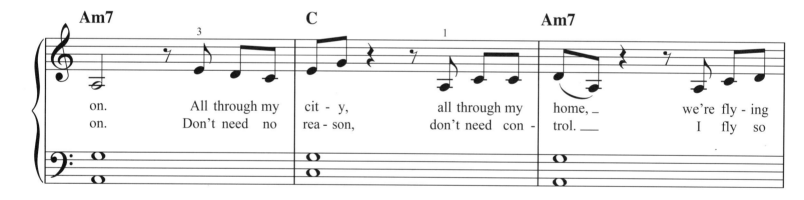

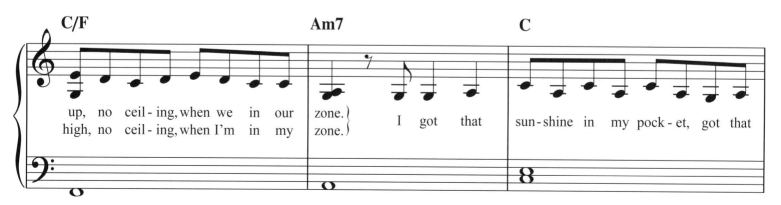

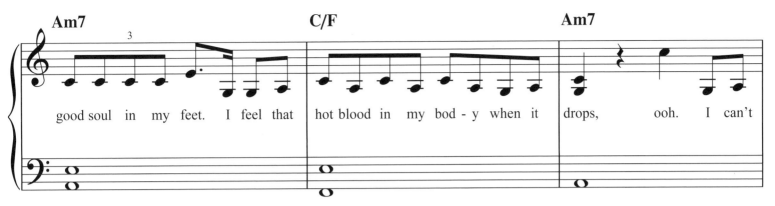

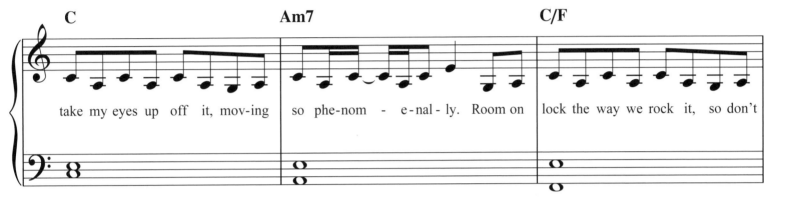

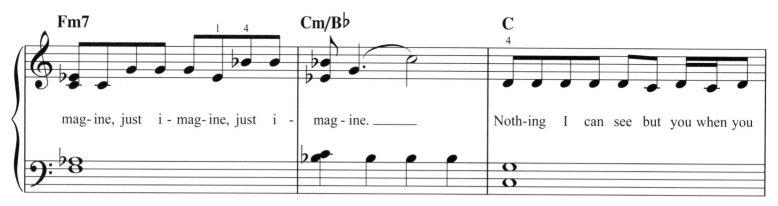

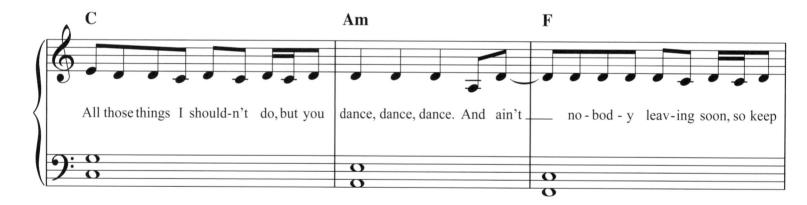

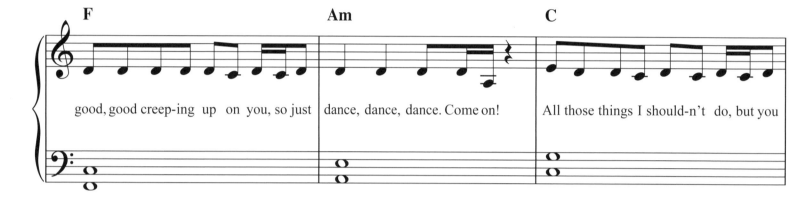

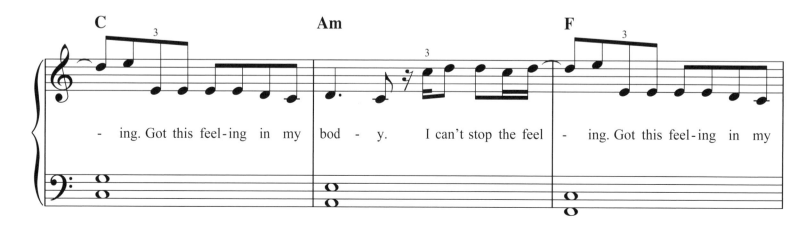

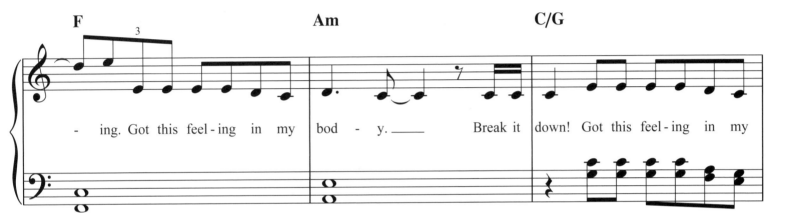

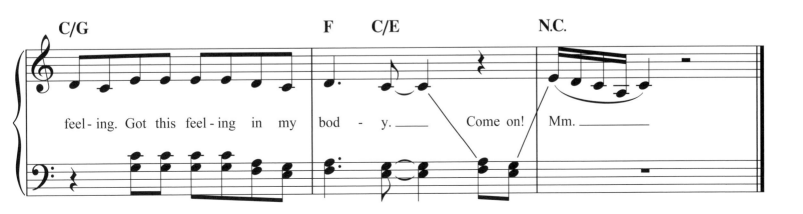

H.O.L.Y.

Words and Music by busbee,
NATE CYPHERT and WILLIAM WIIK LARSEN

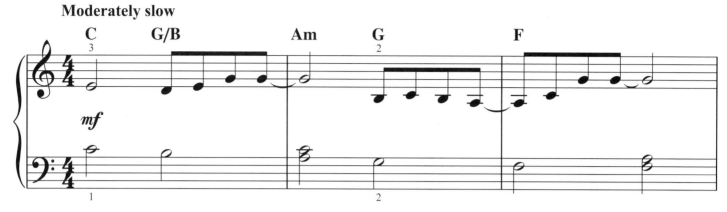

When the sun had left __ and the win-ter came __

and the sky - fall __ could on - ly bring the rain, __ I sat in dark - ness,

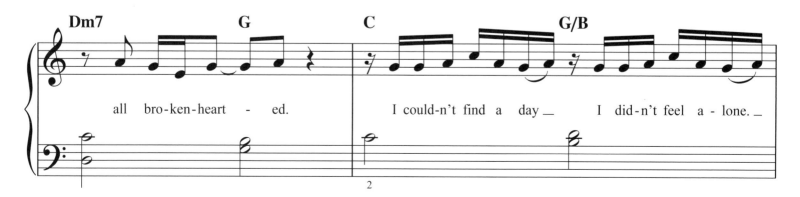

all bro-ken-heart - ed. I could-n't find a day __ I did-n't feel a - lone. __

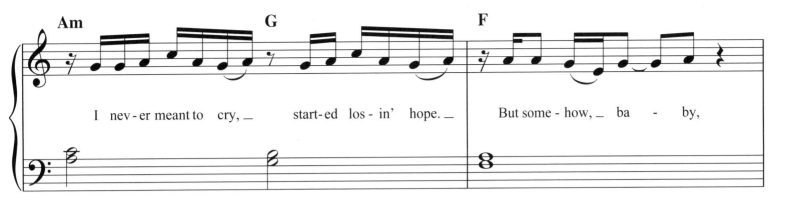

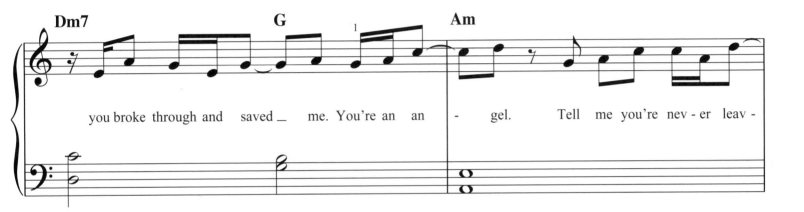

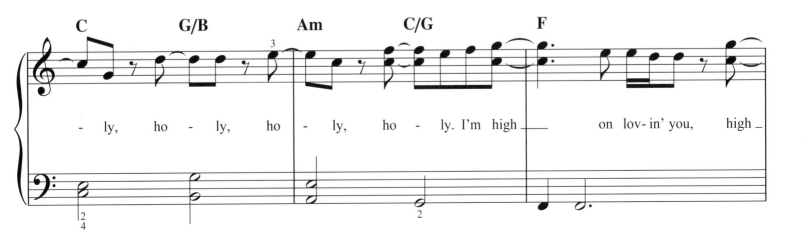

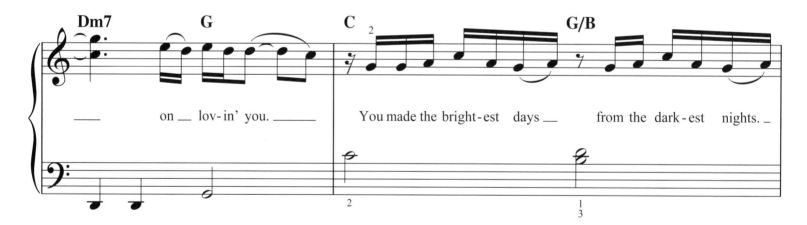

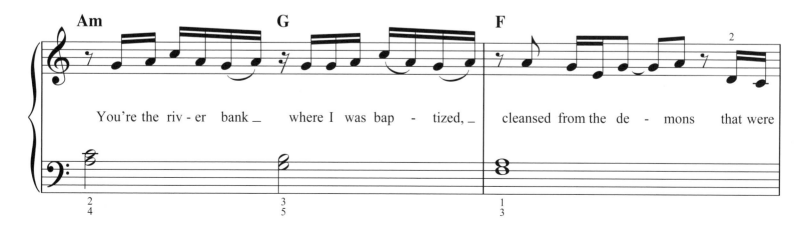

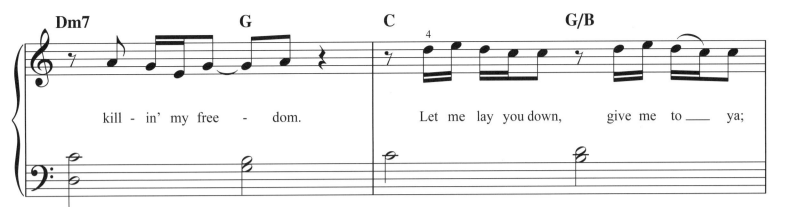

kill - in' my free - dom. Let me lay you down, give me to ___ ya;

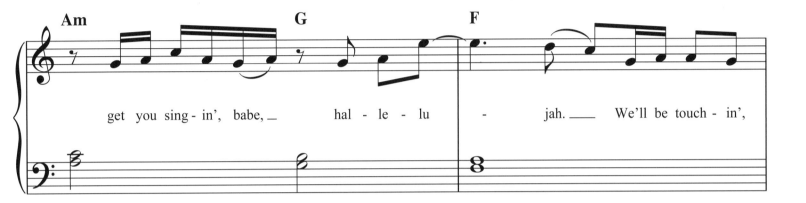

get you sing - in', babe, __ hal - le - lu - jah. ___ We'll be touch - in',

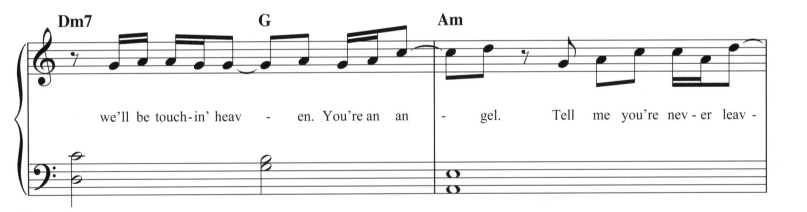

we'll be touch - in' heav - en. You're an an - gel. Tell me you're nev - er leav -

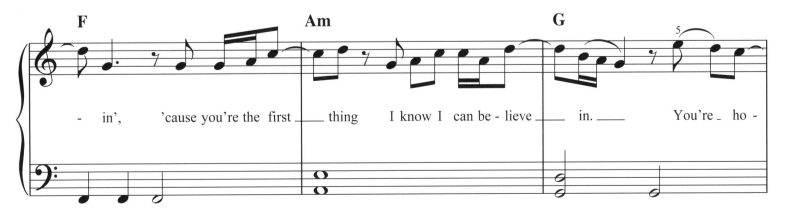

- in', 'cause you're the first ___ thing I know I can be - lieve ___ in. ___ You're ___ ho -

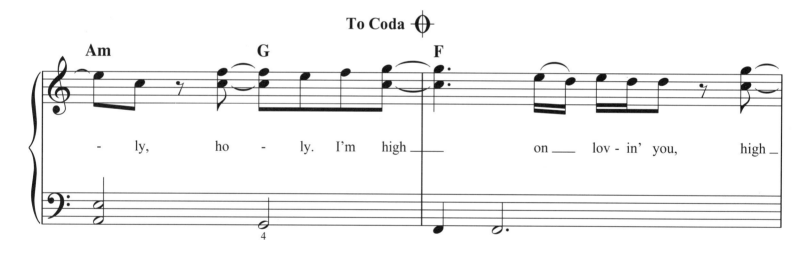

LOST BOY

Words and Music by
RUTH BERHE

Moderately

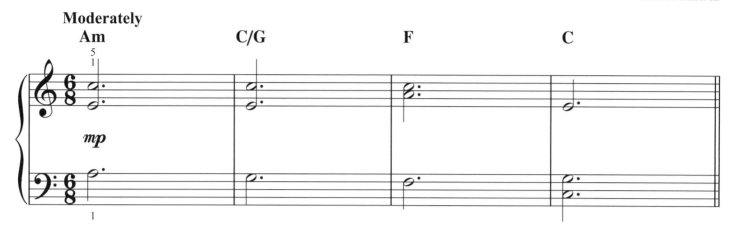

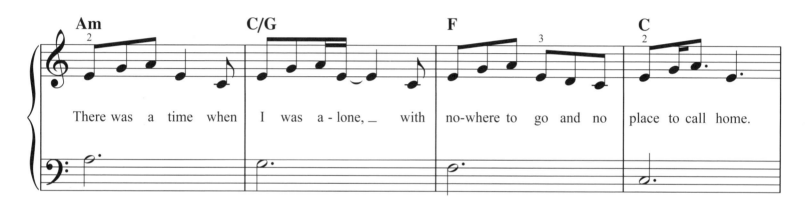

There was a time when I was a-lone, _ with no-where to go and no place to call home.

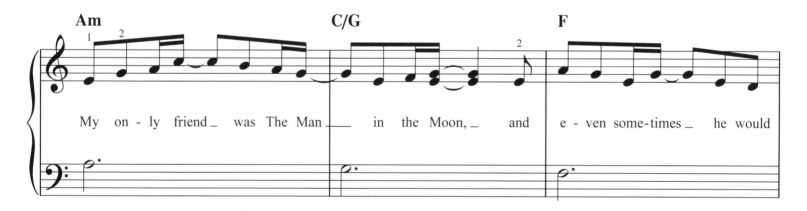

My on-ly friend _ was The Man _ in the Moon, _ and e - ven some-times _ he would

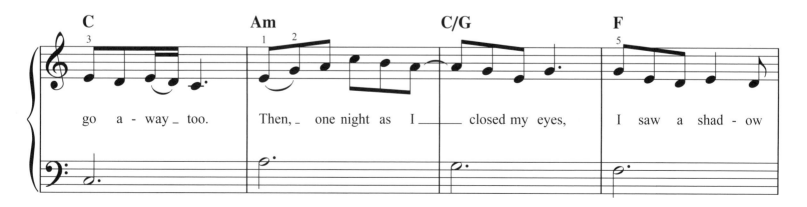

go a - way _ too. Then, _ one night as I _____ closed my eyes, I saw a shad - ow

fly - ing ___ high. He came to me with the sweet - est smile;

told me he want - ed to talk ___ for a - while. _ He said, "Pe - ter Pan,

that's what they call me. I prom - ise that you'll nev - er be lone - ly." And

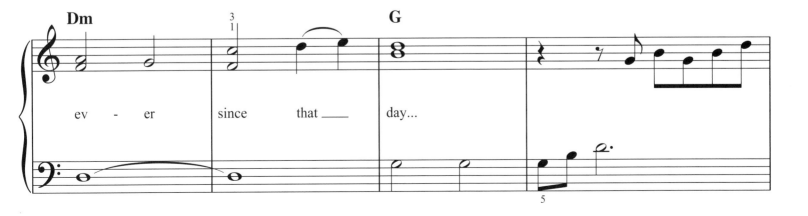

ev - er since that ___ day...

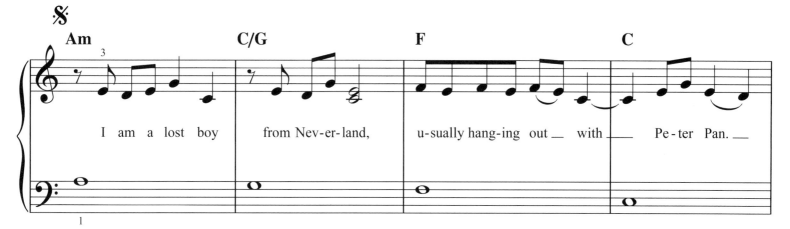

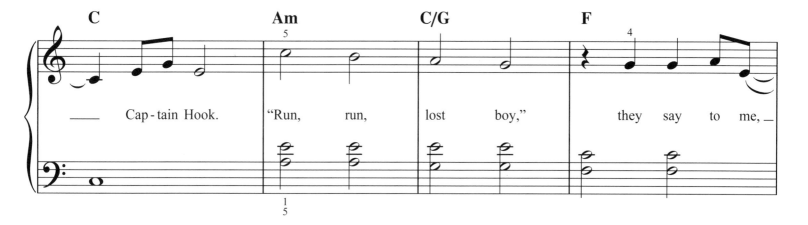

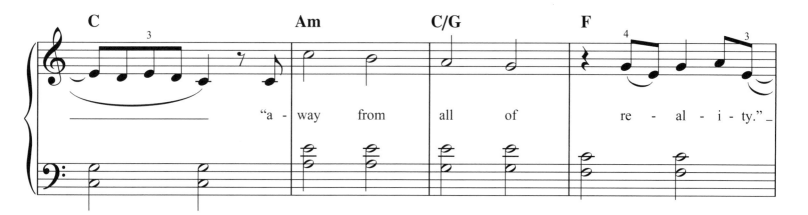

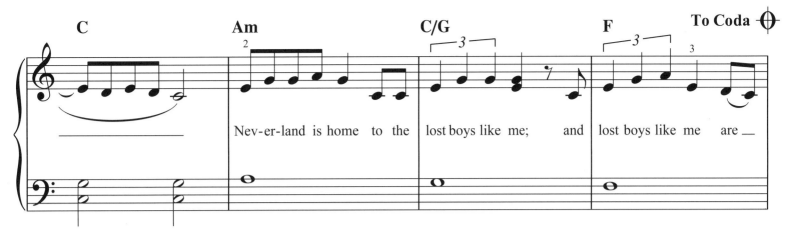

Nev-er-land is home to the lost boys like me; and lost boys like me are ___

free. He sprin-kled me in pix - ie dust and told me to be - lieve, be -

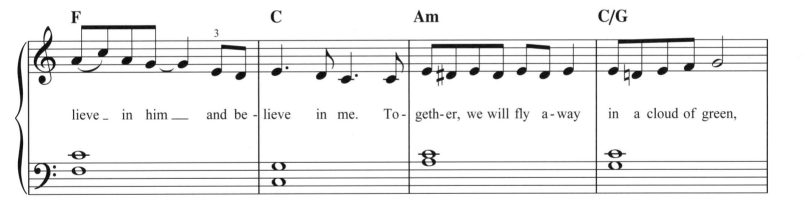

lieve _ in him ___ and be - lieve in me. To - geth-er, we will fly a - way in a cloud of green,

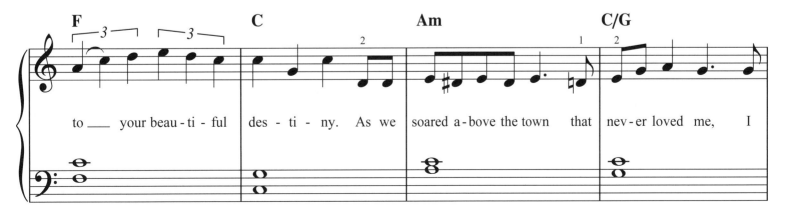

to ___ your beau - ti - ful des - ti - ny. As we soared a - bove the town that nev - er loved me, I

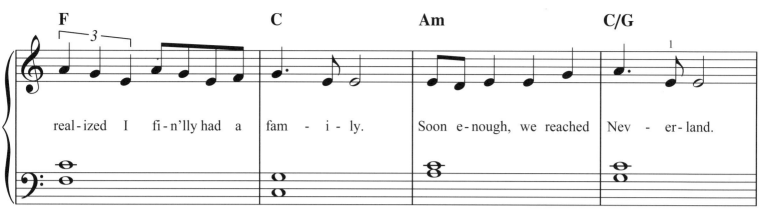

real-ized I fi-n'lly had a fam - i - ly. Soon e-nough, we reached Nev - er-land.

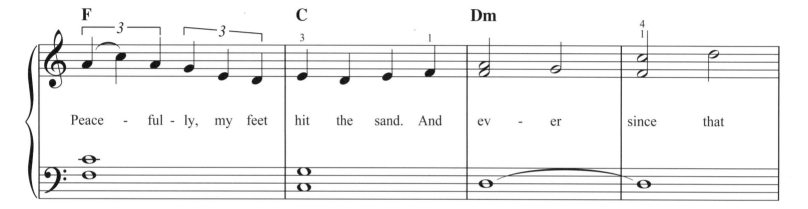

Peace - ful-ly, my feet hit the sand. And ev - er since that

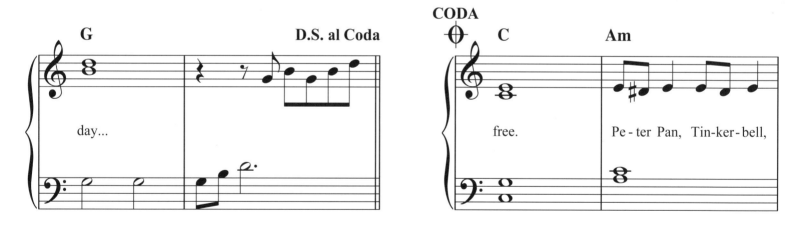

day... free. Pe - ter Pan, Tin-ker-bell,

Wen - dy Dar - ling, e - ven Cap - tain Hook: you are my per - fect sto - ry - book.

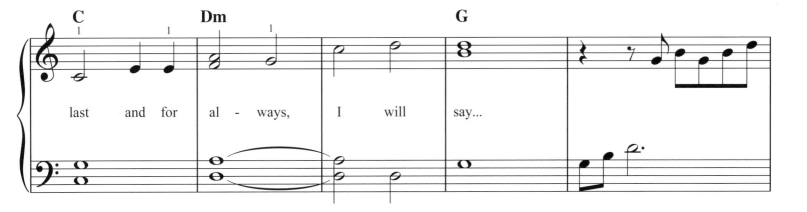

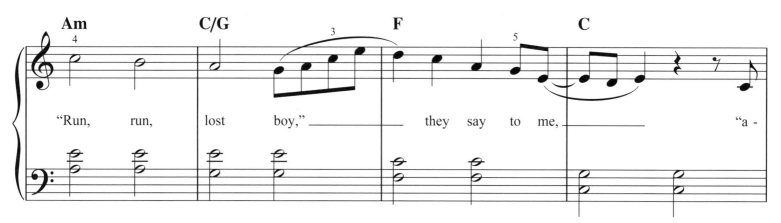

"Run, run, lost boy," they say to me, "a-

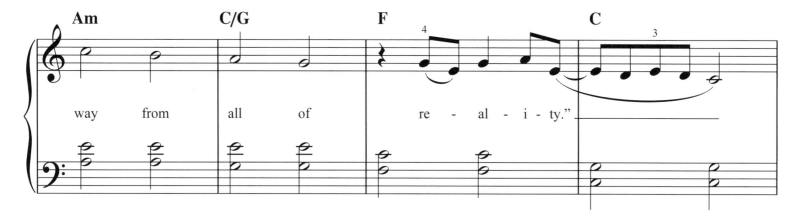

way from all of re - al - i - ty."

Nev-er-land is home to the lost boys like me; and lost boys like me are free.

Nev-er-land is home to the lost boys like me; and lost boys like me are free.

JUST LIKE FIRE
from ALICE THROUGH THE LOOKING GLASS

Words and Music by ALECIA MOORE,
MAX MARTIN, SHELLBACK
and OSCAR HOLTER

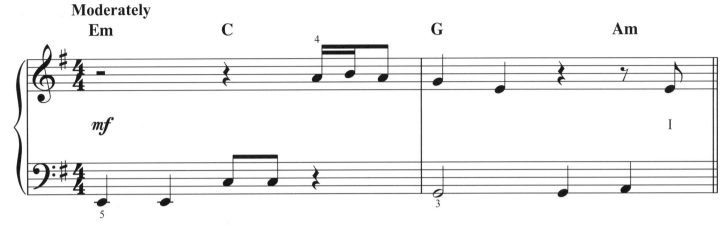

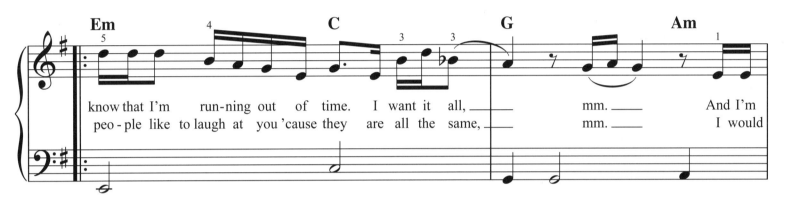

know that I'm run-ning out of time. I want it all, ___ mm. ___ And I'm
peo-ple like to laugh at you 'cause they are all the same, ___ mm. ___ I would

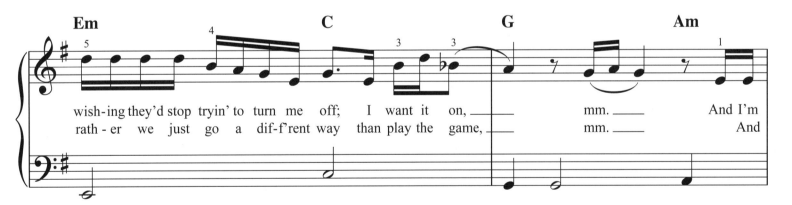

wish-ing they'd stop tryin' to turn me off; I want it on, ___ mm. ___ And I'm
rath-er we just go a dif-f'rent way than play the game, ___ mm. ___ And

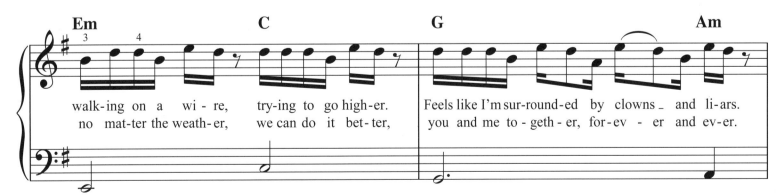

walk-ing on a wire, try-ing to go high-er. Feels like I'm sur-round-ed by clowns _ and li-ars.
no mat-ter the weath-er, we can do it bet-ter, you and me to-geth-er, for-ev - er and ev-er.

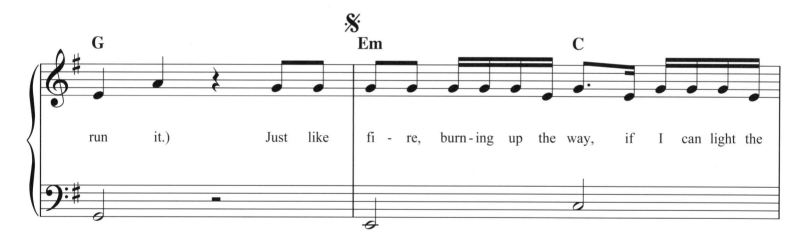

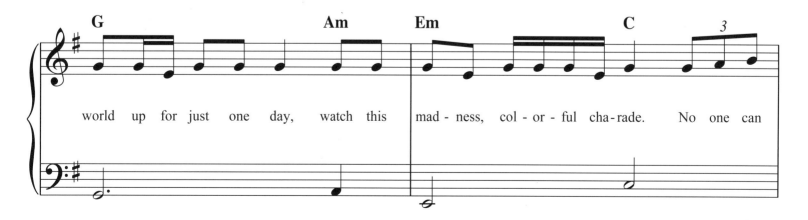

be just like me an - y - way. Just like mag - ic, I'll be fly - ing free. I'm - a dis - ap -

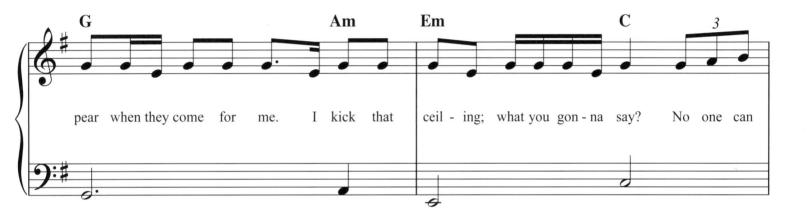

pear when they come for me. I kick that ceil - ing; what you gon - na say? No one can

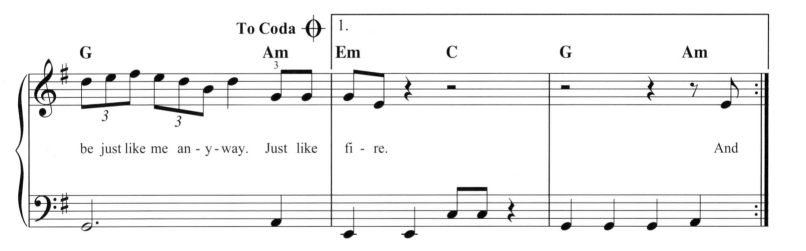

To Coda ⊕ | 1.

be just like me an - y - way. Just like fi - re. And

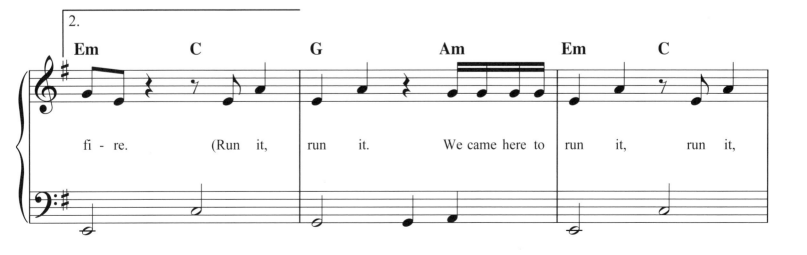

2.

fi - re. (Run it, run it. We came here to run it, run it,

Additional Lyrics

Rap: So look, I came here to run it, just 'cause nobody's done it.
Y'all don't think I could run it, but look, I've been here, I've done it.
Impossible? Please! Watch, I do it with ease.
You just gotta believe. Come on, come on with me.

7 YEARS

Words and Music by LUKAS FORCHHAMMER,
MORTEN RISTORP, STEFAN FORREST,
DAVID LABREL, CHRISTOPHER BROWN
and MORTEN PILEGAARD

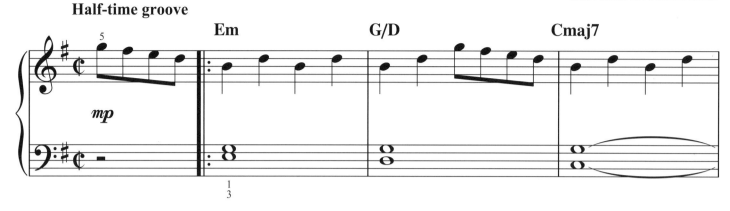

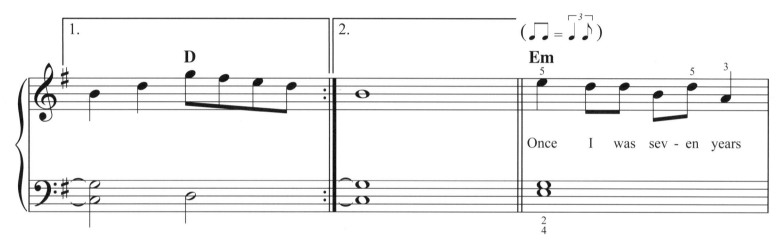

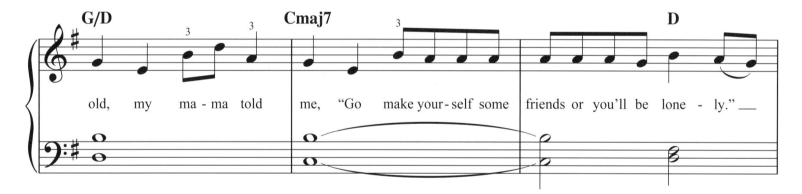

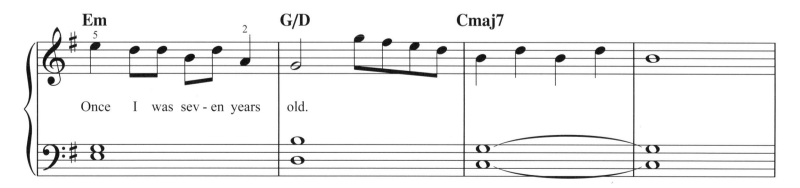

It was a big, big world, but we thought we were big - ger. Push-ing each oth - er to the

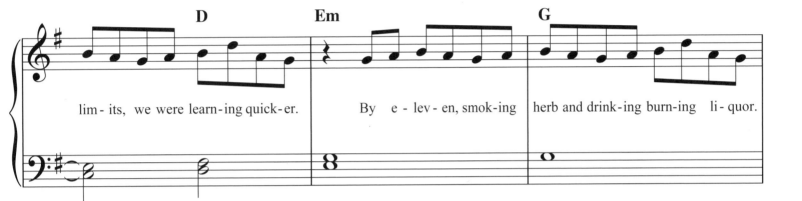

lim - its, we were learn-ing quick-er. By e - lev - en, smok-ing herb and drink-ing burn-ing li - quor.

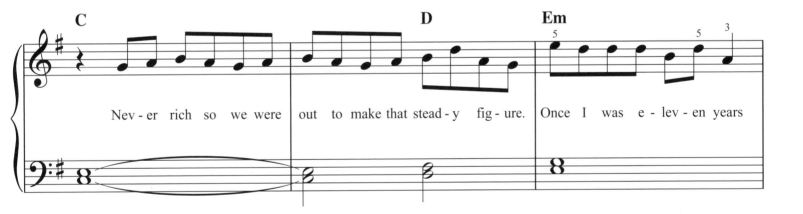

Nev - er rich so we were out to make that stead - y fig - ure. Once I was e - lev - en years

old, my dad - dy told me, "Go get your-self a wife or you'll be lone - ly." __

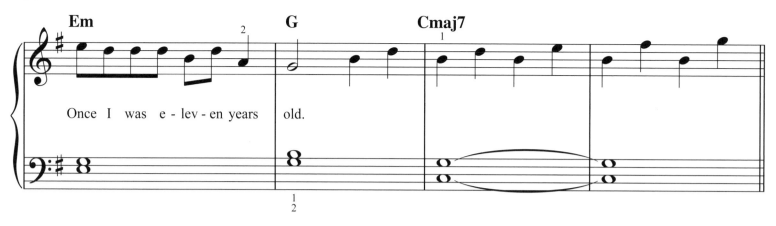

Once I was e - lev - en years old.

I al - ways had that dream like my dad - dy be - fore me, so I start - ed writ - ing
I on - ly see my goals, I don't be - lieve in ___ fail - ure 'cause I know the small - est

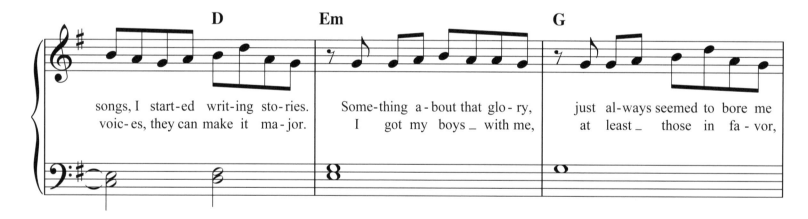

songs, I start - ed writ - ing sto - ries. Some - thing a - bout that glo - ry, just al - ways seemed to bore me
voic - es, they can make it ma - jor. I got my boys ___ with me, at least ___ those in fa - vor,

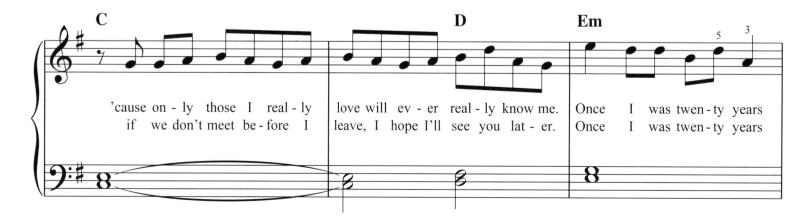

'cause on - ly those I real - ly love will ev - er real - ly know me. Once I was twen - ty years
if we don't meet be - fore I leave, I hope I'll see you lat - er. Once I was twen - ty years

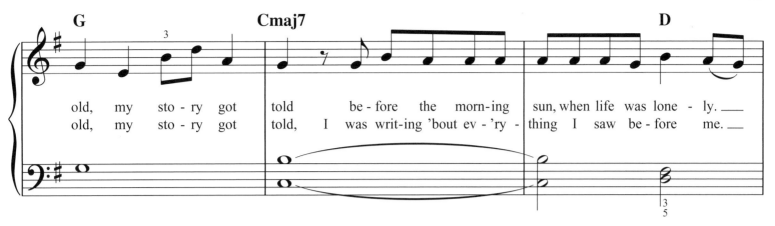

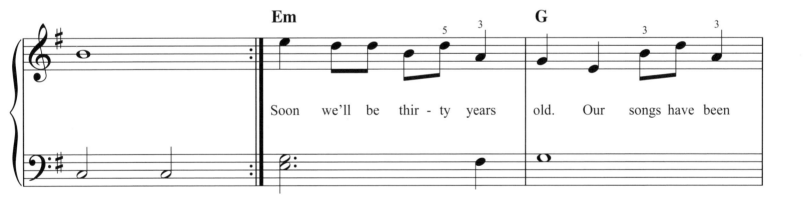

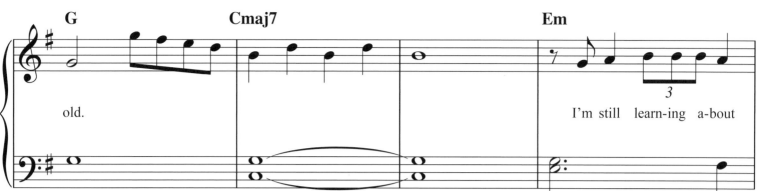

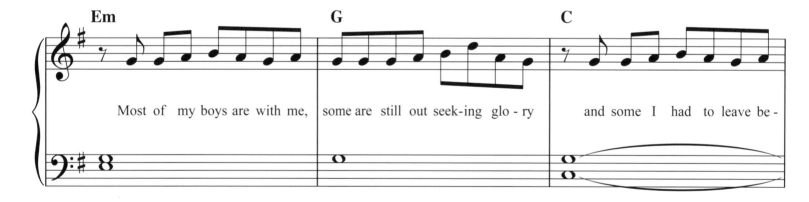

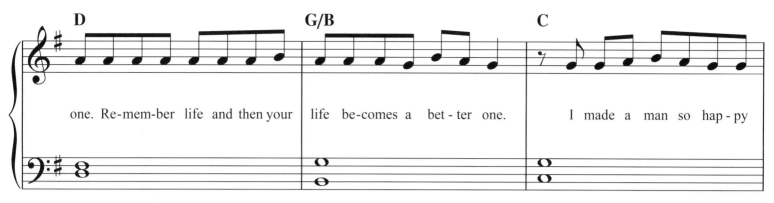

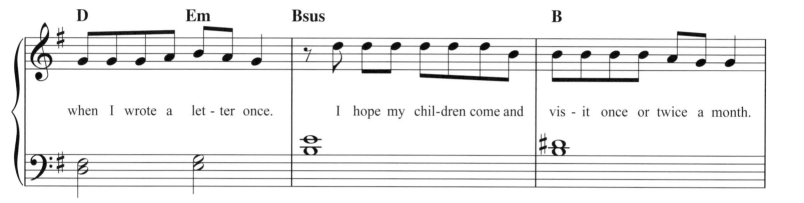

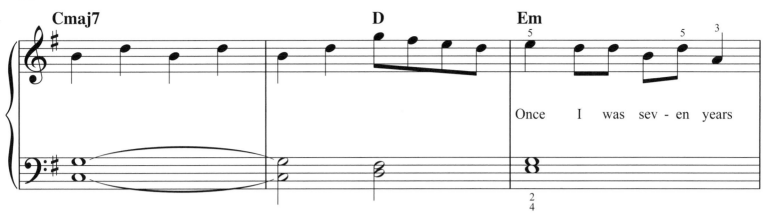

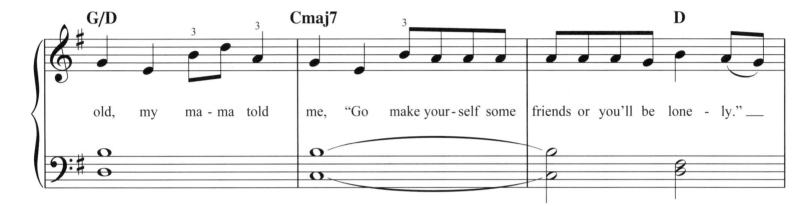

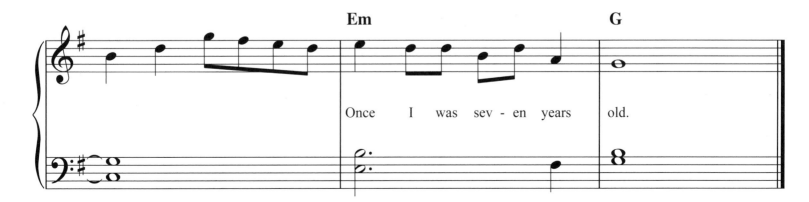